HANDBOOK *for the*

Congregational School Board Member

by **Abraham E. Millgram**

Educational Director,
United Synagogue of America

United Synagogue Commission
on Jewish Education

New York 5713 · 1953

FOR MY SON *Hillel*

CONTENTS

7

One of the slogans of American public education is "the school belongs to the people." This slogan applies equally to the Jewish school. Jewish education should not be relegated solely to the domain of the professional educators, however excellent their qualifications. The interests of our children and of the Jewish community will be best served if Jewish education is planned and guided by a partnership consisting of an informed and devoted lay board, a well trained and consecrated professional faculty, and a wide-awake and interested body of parents.

Many pedagogic tracts have been written for educators; some have been written for parents; but none for the Jewish School Board member. This Handbook, published for the forgotten member of the above-mentioned partnership, is a pioneer in the field of Jewish education. It is the first of its kind.

The author and The United Synagogue Commission on Jewish Education earnestly hope that every congregation will present a copy of this Handbook to each member of its School Board, and that every school administrator, be he the rabbi or the principal, will arrange for the School Board to discuss each section of the Handbook at School Board meetings. Such discussion will generate a greater understanding of the school's goals, of its administrative procedures and of the role of the School Board. The children and the Jewish community will be the beneficiaries of this practice.

In preparing this Handbook, the author received inestimable assistance from many educators. The Readers appointed by the Commission examined the manuscript critically and gave the author valuable guidance. The Readers were Dr. Azriel Eisenberg, Rabbi George Ende, Dr. Simon Greenberg, Dr. Louis Katzoff and Mrs. Israel Oseas. The author is deeply indebted to all the Readers for their criticisms which contributed immeasurably to the publication. The author is also indebted to the members of the Committee on Textbook Publications, especially to its devoted chairman, Mr. Henry R. Goldberg. The members of this committee read the manuscript and submitted written reports containing many constructive suggestions.

Not least is the author's indebtedness to the United

Synagogue Commission on Jewish Education and to its chairman, Rabbi Elias Charry, who has taken a keen interest in this publication. The Commission spent the major part of two meetings discussing the manuscript and clarifying the Commission's stand on several controversial issues.

Since the author is also the editor of the Commission's publications, he felt that it was not proper for him to edit his own manuscript. The Commission graciously complied with his wish and appointed an editorial committee consisting of Mr. Henry R. Goldberg, Rabbi Harold Kastle and Rabbi Abraham Simon. This committee contributed a number of editorial improvements for which the author is deeply grateful.

Despite the valuable contributions of so many educators and rabbis, the School Board member will no doubt still find some inadequacies. For these and for other shortcomings the author alone is responsible.

A. E. M.

Why School Boards Are Necessary

Most Conservative congregations have assumed the responsibility of providing a Jewish education for the children of both members and non-members. The Synagogue Boards, however, are preoccupied with many congregational problems and have not the time to devote to the many details inherent in the conduct of a school. They have found it expedient, therefore, to delegate some of their powers to School Committees or School Boards which are expected to deal with the many problems inherent in the running of a good school.

Unfortunately, the functions and powers of these School Boards are usually vague, and many a School Board which starts out with enthusiasm soon finds itself floundering. The inevitable outcome is frustration, followed by a sense of impotence and a state of inactivity.

Equally damaging to the school program is the discomfiture of the professional educator who finds it necessary to administer his school without a lay board. He finds himself confused and helpless; he loses his sense of direction because he is out of touch with the thinking of the people from whom he derives his professional mandate; and he finds himself without support in his efforts to improve and expand the educational program. He often becomes the target of attack by misinformed, though well-meaning laymen, but is unable to defend himself because he is professionally isolated and helpless.

1 *The Vital Role of the School Board*

A well-functioning School Board is the source of the school's dynamic strength. "The tempo of educational change is closely geared to community understanding and appreciation of educational services," says a prominent educator, who concludes that "it is logical to approach the problem of better education through lay participation." It is logical because an informed, functioning lay board makes for a deepening understanding of the school's objectives and ultimately for a working partnership between the lay School Board and the professional staff. It can also interpret the school program to the Synagogue Board, to the parents and to the community, and thus obtain the public cooperation and the financial underpinning so necessary for the maintenance of a good school program.

2 *The Status of the Congregational School Board*

Despite the prevailing vagueness as to the functions and powers of the congregational Shcool Board, its status has risen considerably during the past two decades. This is due largely to two factors. The first is the growth of the congregational school, and the extension of its educational program which now reaches from pre-school to adult education. No longer is the congregational school an activity relegated to the synagogue basement and delegated to the rabbi and cantor. The congregational school is a mature institution with manifold activities and complex problems. Most Synagogue Boards regard the school as the congregation's prime purpose and most hopeful promise. Synagogues are allocating larger budgets for their schools; are increasingly insisting on professional staffs; and are delegating wider powers to their School Boards.

The second factor stems from the nature of the American Jewish community which is no longer a conglomeration of immigrants. It consists largely of native Americans whose roots are deeply sunk in the subsoil of American culture and whose institutional patterns and practices are imperceptibly yet radically influenced by those of the American community.

Accepted practice in the general field of education is based on the American democratic principle that the average layman's opinion and judgment are worthy of a hearing. It is generally accepted that the layman, though he is no professional educator, can yet grasp basic principles when presented by the professional educator and can contribute to the solution of difficult problems. Lay boards have therefore been established in all American cities and counties, and have been given wide fiscal, administrative and curricular powers. Our congregations have been influenced by this American pattern and are evolving similar procedures.

To be sure, the American city and county School Boards are a rich reservoir of successful experience. But the congregational School Boards can tap only a small part of this experience because the congregation is organically different from the city or county, and its School Board is radically different from that of the city or county School Board. However, wherever there is a clear and helpful parallel between the administrative or organizational practices of the American and the Jewish School Boards, it will be pointed up in its logical place in the Handbook.

3 *Objectives of This Handbook*

Since the congregational schools are constantly grow-
ing in number, and since their scope is widening, congregations are increasingly assigning their best leadership
to their School Boards. But the School Board member,
especially the newly appointed and inexperienced member, though deeply interested in his tasks and earnestly
desirous of carrying out his responsibilities, finds himself
confused and discouraged by the vagueness of his powers
and functions. To be sure, he often receives valuable
guidance from his rabbi or his educational director. Nevertheless he feels frustrated because he cannot put his
finger on a concise yet comprehensive statement of his
functions, responsibilities and powers. Nor can he find a
reliable guide to tested procedures and practices, which
might apply to his school situation. It is the objective of
this Handbook to provide that type of statement, and to
be that kind of guide. The writer is aware that the Handbook does not answer all questions or solve all problems.
It merely attempts to chart a path for the congregational
School Board member. Common sense and balanced judgment will do the rest. It is hoped that this Handbook will
help to enlighten and guide the many laymen who devote
themselves generously to the sacred task of cultivating
"the vineyard of the Lord."

Handbook for the
Congregational School Board Member

CHAPTER 1

Functions of the Congregational School Board

Blueprinting the School Program

1 Policy-Making

The primary function of the School Board is that of setting general educational policy. Since some of its decisions require the approval of the Congregational Board, it is of central importance that the School Board regard itself as the interpreter of school policy at Congregational Board meetings. As policy-maker, the School Board concerns itself with a wide variety of problems. The following will serve as examples: The School Board

a Defines the type of school necessary to meet the needs of the children and embody the ideology of the congregation, and presents the plan to the Synagogue Board for its approval.

> EXAMPLE: The rabbi and the educational director or a member of the Board may present a plan involving a change from three sessions to five sessions per week (or vice versa). If the School Board accepts the plan, it brings it to the Congregational Board, presents the reasons for the recommended change and asks for its approval.

b Authorizes and approves the choice of faculty members recommended by the rabbi and the educational director.

> EXAMPLE: The rabbi and the educational director recommend the engagement of two full time professional teachers and one part-time teacher. If the School Board approves the plan, it authorizes the rabbi and the educational director to interview candidates and to present their recommendations to the School Board for approval.

c Passes on the initiation of new school projects.

> EXAMPLE: The educational director and faculty or a group of parents feel that a Parent-Teacher Association should be organized. The educational director, after discussing the project with the rabbi, brings it to the School Board for approval.

d Initiates or approves plans for the alteration of the school building and the purchase of school equipment, and presents its plans to the Synagogue Board for approval.

> EXAMPLE: The educational director and faculty find that there is a need to replace a wall between two rooms with

a movable partition, so that the two rooms can be used both as classrooms and as a synagogue for the Junior Congregation. After consulting with the rabbi, the educational director presents the plan to the School Board. If the latter approves the structural changes, it takes the proposal to the Synagogue Board for final approval.

e Approves or amends the budget prepared by the educational director in consultation with the rabbi, and presents it to the Synagogue Board for approval.

> EXAMPLE: Increased registration necessitates a larger budget for the school. The School Board, passing upon the revised budget, takes it to the Synagogue Board, explains the reasons for the increased budget, and requests the allocation.

f Determines the tuition scale for members' and nonmembers' children and presents it to the Synagogue Board for final approval.

g Determines the salary scale for members of the faculty and for other employees of the school, and presents it to the Synagogue Board for final approval.

These and other policy-making problems come before a functioning School Board, and its decisions constitute the official policy of the school, a policy which the professional staff must implement.

An important corollary of policy-making is that of setting standards and enforcing them. All too frequently well-meaning but inexperienced School Boards unwittingly undermine their own policies by not enforcing the standards resulting from these policies. For example, most Conservative congregational School Boards have established the requirement that all children above eight attend the weekday school. But the professional staff will find it impossible to enforce this regulation unless it has the full support of the School Board. There is always the danger of some parents appealing to the School Board to make exceptions for their children. *It is of vital importance that a School Board, once it sets a standard, maintain it in the face of all pressure.* If the policy proves impractical, the School Board should change it. But while it is in force the School Board must stand behind the school administrator and firmly endorse his efforts to enforce the rule impartially.

Among the many standards that a School Board is called upon to establish, one may list the following:

a That the one-day-a-week school be limited to children under the age of eight.

b That candidates for Bar Mitzvah and Bat Mitzvah be eligible for the full synagogue ceremony only if they have attended the weekday Hebrew school for a minimum of three years. (In this case the consent of the Ritual or Service Committee will be necessary, since a synagogue ritual is involved as well as the school program.)

c That only students who have passed their fifteenth birthday before January first preceding Shavuot and have attended the weekday Hebrew school a minimum of five years be eligible for the Confirmation ceremony.

d That the school engage only teachers who are graduates of a recognized Hebrew teachers training school or are licensed by an accredited Bureau of Jewish Education.

e That the school adhere to all the school regulations agreed upon by the congregational schools of the community. These might include the following:

1 Rules governing teachers salary scale, vacations and tenure.

2 Rules concerning the school calendar, in which are included the registration period, school opening, school holidays, and school closing for the summer vacation.

3 Regulations governing interschool activities and standards for awards.

f That administrative procedures be enforced without fear or favor. Some schools have in force the following procedures:

1 That no child be admitted after the close of the registration period.

2 That lateness be penalized, and that the penalty be defined and made known to the parents.

3 That a tuition fee be charged for all pupils except those who are economically unable to meet the payments, and that a method be established to determine such inability to pay.

4 That a registration fee be charged, for which the pupil is to receive all his textbooks and supplies.

5 That full salary be paid to teachers on sick leave for a stated period of time.

6 That a specified number of fire drills be scheduled.

In order to enforce school standards it is imperative that the School Board pursue the following procedures:

a School matters affecting congregational policy should be reported to the Congregational Board and should receive the Board's approval.

b The School Board should enforce the regulations without favoritism.

c Where exceptions are necessary, the rules should be so framed that no one can interpret these exceptions as favoritism or laxity, or as an indication of change of administrative policy.

2 Appraising the School Program

A good School Board knows its school. It knows the school's goals, curriculum and organization. But neither the School Board nor its executive arm, the educational director, is infallible. Hence the need of periodic reevaluation of the Board's policies and of the manner of their execution. Furthermore, research, experience, or new conditions may necessitate changes in policy. However, the School Board members, being laymen, must necessarily rely on qualified educators for such evaluation.

Since the School Board is the judge of its own policies and of the effectiveness of the staff, it is all the more imperative that it exercise this power of evaluation with understanding and patience. The Board must learn to distinguish between major and minor failings and must not expect the impossible. Neither should the Board regard its function of appraisal as a means of faultfinding. Rather it should regard this function as an opportunity for discovering the praiseworthy aspects of the school program.

In arranging for a school appraisal the rabbi, the educational director and the faculty should be involved in the planning. It should be a cooperative effort, with the best interests of the children as the objective.

Just as the School Board should not expect the impossible from the faculty, so should it not expect the impossible from the consultant of the local Bureau or from any other educator engaged to appraise the school. No educator can report on the school program after a single visit. A proper appraisal of the school often involves several observation visits, as well as the administration of standardized tests.

When the evaluation of the school is completed, the School Board as well as the faculty should carefully study the report and plan the implementation of its recommendations. This will usually involve long-range planning as well as patient interpretation to Congregational Board members and parents. But it is a good investment of energy. It pays high educational dividends.

If a School Board decides upon a thorough evaluation of its school, it should communicate with the United Synagogue Commission on Jewish Education. The Educational Director of the Commission will advise the Board on how to initiate such an evaluation and will recommend an expert to implement it.

3 Self-Education

The American democratic principle which places faith in the layman's ability to comprehend basic ideas, evaluate them and legislate policy, assumes the layman's concern for the best interests of the institution and its basic goals. It can be assumed therefore that the lay School Board member will approach his work with an open mind and welcome the rabbi's and the educational director's efforts to enlighten him in all matters affecting the educational program of the school. He must always be alert to the mastery of everything that sheds light on the school's goals, curriculum and administration. It is therefore desirable that School Board members should read the quarterly, *The Synagogue School,* published by the United Synagogue Commission on Jewish Education. The School Board should enter a subscription for each member. It is a sound educational investment. Important articles from other sources should be mimeographed and mailed to Board members.

Many School Boards have instituted the practice of setting aside part of their monthly meeting for the study and discussion of various aspects of the educational program. They often invite interested persons who are not on the School Board, as well as the teaching staff, to participate in these discussions. Other School Boards have found it advisable to organize formal study periods at which no school business is on the agenda. The time is fully devoted to discussions and prepared reports based on reading. These efforts have led to a better understanding of the children and their needs. Among the subjects that School Boards discuss at such meetings or study sessions are stimulating articles culled from educational magazines, reports of what is going on in the better, or what some have called "lighthouse schools," and whether the new practices are applicable to their own schools.

CHAPTER 2

Functions of the Congregational School Board

Implementing the School Program

1 *Financing the School*

One of the basic functions of a School Board is to adopt the school budget and obtain the necessary funds for the implementation of the school program.

The school budget should be prepared by the educational director. He should obtain the rabbi's approval and then present the budget to the School Board. The latter should discuss it and, after adopting it, bring it to the Congregational Board meeting. The budget should contain a statement of the anticipated expenditures and incomes during the coming fiscal year. The anticipated expenditures should take into account the following items:

1 Salaries (principal, teachers, substitutes, clerical help)

2 Pensions and insurance payments

3 Books, supplies and materials of instruction

4 Holiday observances, entertainments, etc.

5 Transportation (buses, repair, gasoline, etc.)

6 Office and school equipment (furniture, audio-visual equipment, etc.)

7 Office and miscellaneous expenses

8 Reserves (contingency and emergency funds)

Operation and maintenance of the building, capital outlay, fixed charges such as rent and fire insurance, the rabbi's salary are not listed in the school budget. They are usually included in the congregational budget.

The expenditures of the current year, both actual and anticipated, should be listed in a column parallel to that of the anticipated expenditures during the coming year, so as to indicate changes in the anticipated operational set-up. The anticipated income from all sources should be listed. It is also advisable to include "pie graphs" indicating where the monies come from and where they are spent. Appendix A contains a sample school budget.

Experience has shown that it is wise to establish a wide financial base for the school. The popular adage warning against putting all eggs in one basket does not apply to the public school system, because its basket is insured. By having the power to tax, the city and county School Boards can always secure the funds that are necessary to maintain their schools. The Jewish School Board, however, not having this power, must rely on more than one source of income in order not to be faced with the catastrophe resulting from the collapse of an only source of income. Despite the fact that the Synagogue Board usually regards the school as the chief asset of the congregation, it is quite conceivable that in a year of financial stress, or with the coming to power of an economy-minded administration, the school budget might be drastically cut. If the School Board relied solely on the funds allotted to it by the Synagogue Board, it might be faced with the task of reducing educational standards, a reduction which might result in the collapse of an educational program developed over a long period of time.

The School Board should therefore derive its funds from the following sources:

a *The Congregational Budget.* When a congregation establishes a school it assumes financial responsibility. To quote the statement on policy issued by The United Synagogue Commission on Jewish Education ("The Objectives and Standards for the Congregational School," p. 22):

No educational program can be adequately financed from tuition fees alone. . . . The congregation must therefore provide out of its general funds the substantial sums necessary for creating a sound financial base for the school.

It is the duty of the School Board to present the annual school budget to the Congregational Board, to interpret it and to plead for its adoption. The School Board should exert all its influence and press for the allotment of the "substantial sums necessary." The size of that allotment is determined by local conditions. It ranges from 25% in some congregations to as much as 80% in others.

b *Tuition Fees.* The American pattern provides for free schooling. But this is only a fiction. Everybody pays tuition in the form of taxes. The American system, however, makes education a public responsibility. Hence, people who do not have children in school bear the financial burden along with those who do. But this system is not practical for the Jewish school because the School Board lacks the power of taxation. Experience has shown that the fiscal needs of the school are more adequately met where tuition fees are charged. Not only does the parent contribute more but the money is earmarked for the school and cannot be diverted to other congregational needs.

In establishing tuition rates the School Board should set a higher rate for non-members' children. The justification for this differential is that members are already making a contribution to the school through their membership dues.

The amount of tuition depends largely on local conditions. Whereas some congregations charge no tuition fees for members' children, others charge an annual tuition for all children. The amount of tuition differs greatly. Some affluent congregations charge as much as $75 to $100 per child, payable in advance or in two semi-annual installments; less affluent congregations charge as little as $25, payable in monthly installments. The rates are based not on the quality of the educational program but on the parents' ability and training to pay. The School Board should evaluate the local situation and establish its tuition fees accordingly.

The School Board should also provide for children whose parents cannot or will not pay. Under no circumstances should a child be denied a Jewish education because his parents cannot or will not assume that responsibility. In most synagogues the affiliated organizations, especially the Sisterhoods, establish tuition scholarships for such children.

c *Registration Fees.* "The Objectives and Standards for the Congregational School" (p. 20), recommends that "textbooks should be made available to all pupils at the beginning of the term. Their cost should be defrayed from an annual registration fee or should be included in the tuition." This is a wise policy, followed by most schools. A parent does not object to the payment of a registration fee of $5 per child, for which the school supplies textbooks and other materials. This arrangement makes it possible for all children to receive their books at the beginning of the semester. It also eliminates the confusion resulting from the collection of paltry sums, and saves time spent in collecting these monies and keeping records. What is also important is that the registration fee usually provides enough of a surplus to pay for additional materials, such as teachers' reference books. Some schools have been able to finance their visual aid program from registration fees alone.

d *Community Subsidies.* Since it is the aim of the congregational school to prepare the child not alone for congregational affiliation but also for participation in Jewish communal life, it is incumbent upon the community to assume some of the financial responsibilities of the school. Some communities have therefore seen fit to grant subsidies to such congregational schools as meet the standards established by the Bureaus of Jewish Education in those communities. In Los Angeles the Bureau pays part of the teachers' salaries. In New Haven, Connecticut, there is a more complicated but more practical plan, based on a per capita payment. Such an arrangement not only strengthens the financial base of the school but creates a sounder relationship between the congregational school and the Bureau. It usually results in higher educational standards without infringing on the school's autonomy. (For a detailed description of the New Haven plan, see *The Synagogue School,* Vol. VII, No. 2, November 1948.)

The Congregational Board should bring this matter to the attention of the community for the purpose of securing a reasonable part of the school budget from the general community funds.

e *Miscellaneous Sources.* It is altogether wise for the School Board to encourage the affiliated congregational organizations, such as the Sisterhood, the Men's Club, the Parent-Teacher Association, and, if possible, even the Young People's League, to make contributions to the school program. These contributions should be preferably in the form of scholarships for non-tuition pupils, of subsidies for holiday celebrations, of equipment for audio-visual aids, etc. The affiliated organizations might also provide scholarships for sending children to Camp Ramah, to Leaders Training Fellowship *Kinusim,* or United Synagogue Youth conferences. In general, it can be said that *the more the affiliated organizations are involved in school matters and the greater the number of people who have a stake in the educational program, the better it is for the school.*

f *School Board Projects.* Although the School Board is not a fund-raising agency, it is nevertheless wise for the Congregational Board to delegate fund-raising powers to it so that in time of emergency the School Board may not find itself altogether helpless. During the depression of the early thirties one school in Eastern Pennsylvania managed to maintain its high educational standards. The secret of that success stemmed from the power delegated by the congregation to the School Board to resort to independent fund-raising to meet the emergency. The School Board rallied its friends and conducted a fund-raising affair which saved the school program from sudden collapse. Since the depression continued for several years, the School Board repeated its fund-raising effort annually and thus maintained the school's standards during those trying years. "The Objectives and Standards for the Congregational School" therefore contains the recommendation that the congregation "must empower the School Board to raise additional funds whenever necessary so that the school budget might be adequate for the proper conduct of the school in accordance with the standards herein set forth" (p. 22).*

2 Developing a Good Faculty

Among the functions of a School Board there is none so important as that of developing a good faculty. This function should not be regarded as seasonal in nature. It is an on-going and unending task. No faculty is ever so completely developed as to need no further attention from the School Board. Neither may a faculty be allowed to deteriorate one year in the hope of rebuilding it the next. It takes many years of continued effort to develop a good faculty. But it takes only one season to undermine it. In order to develop a good faculty the School Board must bear in mind the following fundamental principles:

a No school can function properly with substandard personnel. A professional staff is therefore indispensable. Part time teachers, even though they are professional educators in the public school system, cannot give more

* Some School Boards have developed additional sources of income by (1) publishing a School Year Book with advertisements that yield a profit, (2) establishing a scholarship fund deriving its income from individual donors who wish to afford a Jewish education to needy children, (3) setting up a *Yizkor* Fund deriving its income from donations by people who wish to memorialize their departed during the holiday services.

than marginal time and attention to the Jewish school. That is not enough.

b No teacher will stay in a school for any length of time unless (1) the salary provides him and his family with an adequate livelihood, (2) he feels reasonably secure and (3) he feels socially accepted.

c Volunteer teachers should never be accepted even in a one-day-a-week school. It is advisable to insist that the volunteer teachers accept at least a token salary. If they are financially well-to-do, let them return these token salaries as donations. Experience has proven that, with very few exceptions, volunteers weaken the morale and the standards of a school.

But these conditions cannot be met so long as the congregational school can provide its teachers with only part time work, i.e., about ten teaching hours per week. The concept of what constitutes the Hebrew teacher's professional responsibilities must therefore be radically revised. The professional designation of "Hebrew Teacher" should be supplanted by "Jewish Educational Worker." And the scope of the work should be correspondingly widened so as to provide the teacher with an amount of educational work worthy of a salary commensurate with his professional status. The Hebrew teacher, in addition to teaching in the Hebrew school, should engage in one or more of the following activities:

a Extra-curricular activities such as junior congregation, junior choir, arts and crafts, *tefilin* club, library club, Oneg Shabbat groups, school newspaper, etc.

b Youth activities with United Synagogue Youth, Leaders Training Fellowship and Young People's League groups.

c Adult education activities such as administering the congregation's Institute for Adult Jewish Studies, teaching adult classes, or Sisterhood study groups.

d Parent education activities such as P.T.A. programming and parent study groups.

To be sure, no person can possibly be an expert in all these fields. But every teacher must regard it as his duty to master some of these activities in order to supplement his classroom teaching with additional educational work and thus enable the School Board to regard him as a full time member of the staff.

The School Board should set up a salary scale which will attract educators on a full time basis and provide them not only with an adequate livelihood but with annual increments up to a pre-established maximum. In order to provide the teacher with at least a minimum of security, the School Board should establish definite rules governing tenure, and should institute pension and retirement insurance. Needless to say, the School Board should make provision for Social Security insurance for every member of the staff. Appendix B lists several Codes of Practice adopted in some of the larger cities. The School Board should obtain one of these Codes and use it as a guide in the development of its own Code. However, it should be borne in mind that the published Codes reflect their local situations. Teachers' salaries vary widely. Hence salary scales should reflect conditions prevailing in the local community.

Finally, the School Board should make sure that members of the faculty develop a sense of belonging in the community. Teachers should be invited to congregational functions and should be encouraged to participate in communal events. Many School Boards have found it worth while to hold an annual dinner at which the members of the faculty are the guests of honor. At such a dinner the Board has an opportunity to tell the faculty how warmly its devotion and achievements are appreciated.

Another aid in the development of a good faculty is a program of in-service training. Teachers all too humanly tend to fall into a rut. They become professionally stagnant and grow less effective in their educational activities. In larger cities in-service courses are usually given by the local Bureaus of Education and by teacher training schools. In smaller towns the educational director might invite educators from the faculties of nearby teachers colleges and from the ranks of Jewish educators in nearby cities. These educators can offer courses which will help the teacher grow professionally. It is advisable for School Boards to obligate the teachers contractually to participate in the in-service courses and thus keep abreast with developments in the field of education.

CHAPTER 3

Functions of the Congregational School Board

Interpreting the School Program

The School Board is the liaison not only between the school and the congregation but also between the school and the affiliated organizations, the parents, the United Synagogue Commission on Jewish Education and the local Jewish community. In regard to all of these the School Board must see itself as the official interpreter of the school program and its needs.

1 The Congregation and Its Affiliated Organizations

The School Board must assume the responsibility of rendering regular reports at Congregational Board meetings; it must interpret the school and its activities to the Congregational Board; and it must obtain the moral and financial support that the school requires.

The School Board must also involve all the synagogue organizations in the school program so that they regard the school as "their school" and the children as "their children." The affiliated organizations, especially the Sisterhood and the Men's Club, should be encouraged to sponsor and finance special school projects such as holiday celebrations, junior congregation, Bar Mitzvah breakfasts, as well as the other projects mentioned above (p. 36).

2 The Parents

The School Board should encourage the organization of a Parent-Teacher Association. The basic aims of the organization should be parent cooperation in school activities and the development of a program of parent education. It must be borne in mind that Jewish education which is not carried into the home is academic in nature and therefore ineffective. Through a program of parent education, consisting of study groups, holiday institutes as developed by the National Women's League, and well planned programs at the Parent-Teacher Association meetings, it is possible to exert a healthy influence on the pupils' homes.

Many schools have found it practical to set aside one

week annually as "Open School Week." During that week the parents are invited to visit the classes, meet with the teachers, and become acquainted with the school program as well as their children's progress.

Another project in this area consists of sending monthly letters to the parents, informing them of various phases of the school program and guiding them in the performance of their role in the education of their children. Some congregations also allocate a special section of their bulletin to school news and projects.

The School Board should take time at its meetings to discuss parent education and to plan a program suitable for the local situation.

3 The United Synagogue Commission on Jewish Education

The Commission represents the United Synagogue of America, the Rabbinical Assembly of America and the Teachers Institute of the Seminary. Among the important functions of the Commission are the following:

1 It sets national educational policy for the Conservative congregational schools.

2 Publishes curricula.

3 Publishes textbooks.

4 Publishes a quarterly, *The Synagogue School.*

5 Arranges regional educational conferences.

6 Conducts a placement bureau for teachers and educational directors.

7 Conducts a Foundation School Department.

The School Board should acquaint itself with the Commission's publications. Particularly its statement of policy, "The Objectives and Standards for the Congregational School," should be carefully studied by each member of the School Board, since it represents the official policy of the Conservative Movement. It should be discussed at School Board meetings with a view to implementing its recommendations.

The School Board should also acquaint itself with all other publications of the Commission—curricula and textbooks—and should explore their potential usefulness to the school.

Finally, the School Board should give fullest cooperation to the Commission in the implementation of all projects sponsored by the Commission. The Commission exists by virtue of the service it can render the congregational schools individually and collectively. Letters from the Commission should be read at School Board meetings and should, so far as possible, be acted upon. Educational conferences sponsored by the Commission should be attended by School Board members, and transactions at such conferences should be discussed at School Board meetings.

The Commission's office is at 3080 Broadway, New York 27, N. Y.

4 *Local Associations of United Synagogue Schools*

In some larger communities there are Associations of United Synagogue Schools, which are functioning under the guidance and in cooperation with the local Bureaus of Jewish Education. The School Board should be represented on the Association's Executive Board, receive reports from its representatives, and in every way cooperate in the projects sponsored by the Association. The success of such projects will inevitably enrich the school's program.

Among the projects sponsored by such Associations are the following:

1 Curriculum workshops

2 Uniform curricular standards

3 Uniform testing program

4 Uniform awards system

5 Uniform school calendar

6 Interschool activities

7 Joint High School

8 Teachers' conferences

5 *The Local Community*

A working relationship should be established with the local Bureau of Jewish Education wherever such a Bureau exists. Much good will result from such mutual co-operation because a well-functioning Bureau can render many valuable services to the school. Among the more important are the following:

1 Consultation leading to improved teaching and administration

2 In-service courses

3 Teachers' conferences

4 Curriculum workshop for the preparation of syllabi and courses of study

5 Uniform testing program

6 City-wide awards system

7 Educational library and visual aids

8 Subsidies for school budget

9 Unified transportation system

10 Periodic surveys

11 Uniform school calendar

12 Interschool activities (assemblies, contests)

13 City-wide Hebrew High School

Appendix C is a joint statement by the United Synagogue Commission on Jewish Education and the American Association for Jewish Education dealing with the basic principles that should guide the relationship between the congregational school and the local Bureau of Jewish Education.

6 Championing the Children's Needs

Despite the universal claim that everyone loves children, there are people who knowingly or unknowingly encroach upon children's needs. In such situations the School Board should regard itself as the defender of the children and the champion of their needs. For example, if the junior congregation holds services in a shabby place while the adult congregation meets in a beautiful synagogue, it is the duty of the School Board to plead the children's cause and to point out to the Congregational Board that the children stand in need of religious inspiration as much as the adults. If the congregational *Sukkah* is needed simultaneously by the children and the adults, the School Board should plead the cause of the children. The School Board must have a genuine love and respect for the children, and should regard itself as the guardian of our "most precious resource."

The education of our children is an exacting task with many duties and responsibilities. It demands the devotion and consecration of those who have been chosen for membership on the School Board. But this work is richly rewarding if members of the School Board regard their task not as a burden but as a unique privilege.

CHAPTER 4

The School Board
and School Administration

One of the basic principles of administration is that of delegation of power. Wise School Boards know their power but choose not to exercise it. By delegating wide administrative powers to the educational director or principal, a School Board contributes greatly to the efficiency of the school and to the morale of its staff.

1 The School Board's Powers

As previously stated, the congregational School Board derives its powers from the synagogue Board of Directors. However, this does not mean that the School Board is a mere intermediary between the Congregational Board and the professional school staff. Wisdom and experience dictate that the synagogue Board of Directors delegate to the School Board wide powers to implement the school program. The Synagogue Board usually reserves for itself the last word in a few basic areas, such as type of school and budget. All others are assumed to be delegated to the School Board. A wise School Board, however, will refer all important matters of policy to the Synagogue Board so as to utilize the Synagogue Board's prestige in the implementation of its own policy.

It should be emphasized that even in areas reserved for the Synagogue Board, the School Board usually plays a decisive role. For example, the School Board does not have the final say in determining the school budget. However, if despite its pleading and pressure the Synagogue Board still finds it necessary to revise the budget, its revisions, as a rule, apply only to the total amount. The School Board is left free to decide where reductions can best be made so as to cause least injury to the school. Similarly, a wise Synagogue Board will not overrule School Board policies. This gives the School Board the feeling that it is, for all practical purposes, autonomous in the exercise of its duties.

2 The Role of the Rabbi

In smaller congregations the rabbi is also the educational director. In larger schools these functions are divided. The exact point at which such a division of respon-

sibility occurs is not easy to determine. "The Objectives
and Standards for the Congregational School," issued by
the United Synagogue Commission on Jewish Education,
establishes the following categorical rule:

> It is assumed that in the average congregation the rabbi
> is the active principal of the school. However, practical ex-
> perience has proved that a school of 200 children or more
> requires more time for its efficient administration than the
> rabbi can normally give. Hence, every effort should be
> made to provide a school of more than 200 pupils with a
> full time principal who possesses adequate academic and
> educational training, and teaching experience to qualify
> him to administer and supervise the school effectively.
> Where a principal is engaged, the rabbi should serve as
> general supervisor of the school, and all planning of poli-
> cies, of curriculum and administration should be subject to
> his approval. The rabbi and the principal should be jointly
> responsible to the School Board for the proper administra-
> tion and supervision of the school.
>
> Where there is no full time principal, a qualified teacher
> should be designated as head teacher. He should carry only
> a part time teaching schedule so that he can assist the
> rabbi with the administration and supervision of the
> school.

The rabbi derives his powers from the congregation
that elected him. He is the spiritual leader and the central executive of all synagogue activities. He is an ex-
officio member of the School Board and acts as its trusted
counsellor. When an educational director is chosen, the
School Board must obtain the rabbi's consent. It is in

this manner that the rabbi and the School Board jointly delegate administrative powers to the educational director. That is one reason why the educational director is expected to clear with the rabbi all important recommendations before bringing them to the School Board. The advantages of this procedure are:

1 The Board is always sure that the recommendations have the joint backing of the rabbi and the educational director. Such a procedure also precludes the development of contradictory policies.

2 The School Board is assured that the recommendations are in consonance with general congregational policy with which the rabbi is usually best acquainted.

3 It guarantees that in all curricular matters the congregation's religious orientation will be given due consideration.

4 School policy thus arrived at will more readily receive the backing of the synagogue leadership, for the rabbi, as a rule, is in the most strategic position to interpret school policy and obtain support for school projects.

5 It leads to a greater involvement of the rabbi in the school program.

It is generally recognized that the rabbi of a large congregation is too busy to devote the major part of his time to the school. Experience, however, indicates the importance of the rabbi's personal contact with the children, a contact which frequently results in lasting bonds. These bonds often flower into lifelong loyalties to the rabbi, to the synagogue and to Jewish values. To establish such contact it is imperative that the rabbi teach at least one class, preferably the Confirmation class.

3 The Role of the Educational Director or Principal

Experience in the general field of education has established the wisdom of making the Superintendent of Schools the central figure in the school system. A wise city or county School Board is generous in delegating wide powers to the Superintendent, thus enabling him to function effectively. Even in the determination of overall policies, a function which the School Board always reserves for itself, the Superintendent of Schools acts as the professional consultant, not only posing the problems at hand but clarifying them and offering specific recommendations.

In the congregational school the educational director or principal should occupy a position similar to that of the Superintendent of Schools. He is the person most immediately concerned with the implementation of school policies and the development of the school program. It is therefore important that he participate in the deliberations which lead to the formulation of policy. He is not a member of the School Board and does not have the right to vote. But he should attend all School Board meetings except when his own status is under discussion. He should be regarded by the School Board and the rabbi as the expert, helping the School Board to reach intelligent decisions, much like an engineer or architect who presents blueprints and explains their implications.

The educational director or principal is also the executive officer of the School Board in all matters of school administration. He is responsible for the implementation of both the educational program and the school's business transactions. These two areas should always be regarded as integral parts of the general school program and should not be thrust into separate categories. The purchase of school supplies is part of the educational director's duties, just as is the implementation of the curriculum. In choosing an educational director, the School Board should be aware of this fact and make its choice on the basis of the candidate's administrative ability in both fields.

To be sure, the School Board is responsible for the program and the administration of the school. But the average School Board member is neither a professional educator, capable of developing a sound school curriculum, nor a trained supervisor, nor a professional administrator equipped with a knowledge of the techniques of school administration. Furthermore, the School Board member does not have the time for the detailed attention that the administration of a school involves. Hence a wise

School Board limits its functions to the exercise of its legislative and appraisal powers. It sets policies and evaluates the manner of their execution.

Just as the effectiveness of the School Board depends, in large measure, on the confidence of the Congregational Board, a confidence which expresses itself in the delegation of wide powers to the School Board, so is the effectiveness of the educational director or principal largely dependent on the wide powers that the School Board delegates to him. The morale of the administrator is a vital factor in the effectiveness of his work. *The School Board should therefore leave administration completely to the professional staff.* If the educational director is incompetent he should be replaced but never reduced to the status of an errand boy.

Among the most important functions of the educational director or principal are the following:

a To carry out the policies and bylaws established by the School Board.

b To serve as executive officer of the School Board in the implementation of its school program and other activities.

c To attend School Board meetings and to participate in all deliberations without the right to vote.

d To make periodic progress reports on the conditions and needs of the school.

e To prepare, for the approval of the School Board, rules and regulations for the direction and control of the school.

f To interpret the school's needs to the School Board.

g To nominate, in consultation with the rabbi, and recommend to the School Board, teachers and other personnel in accordance with the authorization of the School Board; also to recommend for discharge any employee whose services are so unsatisfactory as to warrant such action.

h To organize the school and to assign teachers to the classes.

i To prepare, in consultation with the rabbi and in co-operation with the faculty, the school curriculum.

j To choose, in consultation with the faculty, textbooks and other supplies needed for the implementation of the school curriculum.

k To hold faculty meetings, as part of an on-going teacher training program, and as an aid in the administration of the school.

l To observe teachers in their classrooms and make specific suggestions for the improvement of their teaching techniques.

m To assist the teachers in planning their work, by providing them with curriculum materials such as monthly guides outlining special holiday observances, etc.

n To direct the school and its extra-curricular activities.

o To supervise the maintenance of the school building and its equipment.

p To prepare, in consultation with the rabbi, the annual school budget and submit it to the School Board.

q To direct and supervise all financial affairs of the school, such as the collection of tuitions, implementation of fund-raising projects, etc.

r To approve all purchases and expenditures within the budget, and to make periodic reports of such expenditures.

s To prepare and recommend for the School Board's consideration plans for the alteration of the building or for the construction of a new building.

t To maintain favorable public relations with the parents, the members of the congregation, the local Bureau of Jewish Education, and the national United Synagogue Commission on Jewish Education.

4 *The Ladder of Authority in the Congregational School*

It is important for the efficient administration of a school that there be a clear understanding of the ladder of authority as well as of the major spheres of responsibility in the school. In the public school system there has developed a unitary line of authority which goes from the State Board of Education to the local School Board, to the Superintendent of Schools, to the principal, to the faculty and other school personnel. This unitary line of authority is logical, easily grasped and readily accepted by laymen and professional educators. Unfortunately, the organization of the congregation and of the American Jewish community does not permit the emulation of the public school system in this regard. There are two important factors which play crucial roles in the congregational school but which complicate the line of authority, namely, the rabbi of the congregation and the local Bureau of Jewish Education.

The rabbi is usually a determining force in the school program. He has the best access to the leadership of the congregation, and is in a strategic position when it comes to obtaining congregational support for the school program. His influence is particularly decisive when curriculum and courses of study are under consideration. The school is considerably strengthened by the rabbi's involvement in its program, but his position makes him a collateral factor in the hierarchy of authority. This creates a dualism in authority which can function effectively only if there is unity of purpose on the part of the School Board and the rabbi.

The Bureau of Jewish Education which exists in almost every larger Jewish community also plays an important collateral role in the development of the school program. The Bureau can give not only guidance and supervision to the faculty, but can help the Board evaluate the school program and advise it regarding the extent to which the school program is succeeding. Where the relationship between the Bureau and the School Board is sound, and where mutual faith and good will exist, the School Board's effectiveness can be greatly enhanced by the central agency's advice and guidance.

Despite the absence of a unitary ladder of authority, the organizational channels of the congregational school are not complicated, as can be seen from the following diagram:

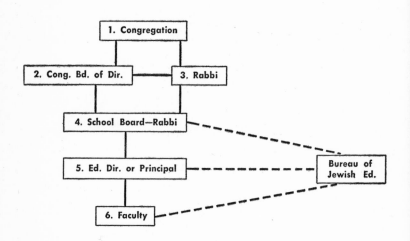

In larger communities where there are Associations of United Synagogue Schools, the Bureau of Jewish Education finds it advantageous to channel most of its services through the Association. The introduction of this additional factor complicates the ladder of authority only slightly as may be seen from the following diagram:

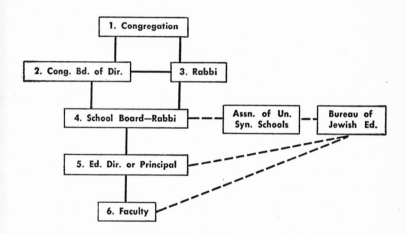

The following outline delineates some of the major spheres of responsibility as they exist in the congregational school

1 Congregation
  a Elects Board of Directors
  b Elects rabbi
  c Delegates power to Board of Directors and to rabbi

2 Congregational Board of Directors
   a Delegates powers to School Board
   b Approves type of school
   c Approves budget

3 Rabbi
   a Administrative head of all departments of congregational activity
   b Trusted counselor to Congregational Board and to School Board
   c Is consulted by principal before submission of plans to School Board

4 School Board
   a Delegates administrative powers to educational director or principal
   b Defines school policies
   c Appraises school program
   d Draws up budget for presentation to Congregational Board

5 Educational Director or Principal
   a Administers school
   b Supervises classroom instruction and school activities
   c Implements policies defined by the School Board
   d Trusted adviser and guide of School Board

6 Bureau of Jewish Education
   a Advises principal and rabbi on curriculum, courses of study and administration of school
   b Provides consultation to teachers on methods of teaching and classroom management
   c Helps School Board to appraise the school program

5 The Relationship Between the Rabbi and the Principal

It is imperative that the rabbi and principal see eye to eye in matters of ideology, curriculum and courses of study. The recommendations previously made in the Handbook that the rabbi nominate the candidate for principal and present his name to the School Board, and that the principal consult with the rabbi on important matters such as budget, salaries, etc., are calculated to assure the harmony necessary for a healthy school climate.

In order that the harmonious relationship between rabbi and principal be built on a solid foundation, it is necessary that the principal accept the fact that the rabbi is the spiritual leader of the congregation and that as such his interests are coextensive with the congregation's activities. This is especially true of the school since it is one of the most important, if not the most important, congregational activity. The rabbi is therefore concerned with the school as a whole as well as with every phase of its program. He should feel free to observe any class and to follow up any phase of the school's activities in which he is especially interested. He should be consulted by the principal on curricular matters and courses of study before the faculty meets to work on the curriculum or on courses of study. In school functions which are tied up with the synagogue service, such as *Hakafot,* consecration of new pupils, confirmation and children's services in the main synagogue, the rabbi's say should be final.

On the other hand, the principal should receive the rabbi's fullest cooperation in the fulfillment of his duties. Without such cooperation the principal's authority is weakened and his efforts are unavailing. Having nominated the principal for the post, it is the rabbi's moral obligation to uphold the principal's hand. The rabbi can render effective assistance in many areas such as the following:

1 Respect the principal's professional prerogatives by not interfering with administrative matters such as organization of classes, classification of pupils, supervision of instruction, choice of textbooks, and daily routines involving forms, schedules, etc.

2 Teach the confirmation class or a high school class or both.

3 Honor faculty recommendations regarding eligibility for confirmation.

4 Help the registration campaign by delivering a sermon on Jewish education during the High Holiday season, and by making appropriate announcements from the pulpit.

5 Cooperate in the organization and programming of a Parent-Teacher Association.

6 Speak or preside at school functions such as holiday celebrations and graduations.

7 Permit the distribution of school leaflets in the synagogue, and publicize school activities in the congregational bulletin.

As a rule harmony and cooperation characterize the relationship between the rabbi and the principal. However, disagreements occasionally occur. Such a situation is serious. The School Board should not permit it to linger in the hope that the problem would in time solve itself. Such situations usually deteriorate and result in each party working against the other to the detriment of the school.

There is no clear cut procedure for School Boards to follow in such matters. The wide variety of irritating situations, clashing personalities, and opposing ideologies makes it impossible to prescribe a course of action applicable everywhere. It can only be urged that the differences between rabbi and principal be aired openly at a School Board meeting and be amicably settled. If the first attempt fails, the School Board should persist until peace and harmony are restored.

6 *Where the Role of the School Board Ends*

Before concluding this chapter, it is important to warn the School Board against a number of pitfalls. There is always the danger of a School Board going beyond its normal functions and of usurping the prerogatives of the educational director and of the faculty. In addition to legislating policy and appraising the school work, many a School Board assumes responsibilities which are professional in nature. It is therefore in place to list a few "don'ts."

a It is not a wise School Board that exercises its policy-making powers without consulting its professional staff. *The rabbi and the educational director should be the trusted advisers of the School Board* in all educational matters. If the School Board does not have faith in its educators it should replace them. But it must not legislate without their guidance and participation.

b Although the School Board is responsible for the execution of its policies, it should never usurp the administrative responsibilities of the educational director. The School Board members are not in a position to perform the executive duties of administration, and the sooner they recognize this fact the better it is for the school. It should therefore be one of the basic policies of the School Board to delegate administrative responsibility to the administrator. This should be clearly recorded in the Board's minutes as a basic rule of procedure.

> *The board legislates; the superintendent executes*—The basic division-of-labor principle, discovered through the experience of those boards and superintendents working together most effectively in the past, is that *legislative* powers and functions shall belong to the board and *executive* powers and functions to the superintendent. This is a principle that has taken much experience, some of it bitter, to reveal. (American Association of School Administrators, "School Boards in Action" in *Twenty-Fourth Yearbook*, 1946, pp. 47-48.)

c Board members have the right to be critical of the curriculum prepared by the rabbi, the educational director and faculty. But they must not constitute themselves into a curriculum committee. If the curriculum presented is not acceptable, the School Board may call in curriculum experts for their recommendations. But the School Board must not usurp the educator's prerogatives in this field.

d It is altogether proper for School Board members to visit classes in session. These visits, however, should be only for the purpose of getting an intimate idea of the school program in action. They should be infrequent, for they tend to disrupt the normal work of the classes; they should be arranged in advance through the educational director or principal; and advance notice of such visits should always be given to the teachers involved. *But School Board members must not visit classes for the purpose of supervising or evaluating the work of the teachers.* Supervision is an educational specialty for which the layman is not equipped. This function must be entrusted to the educational director or principal. If the School Board feels that it needs special guidance or information to enable it properly to appraise the work of the school, it should invite an educator who is recognized as an expert in school appraisal. This educator will visit the classes and report to the School Board.

e *No School Board should undertake to test classes.* Testing is a science in which even educators are not all experts. If the School Board feels that testing is needed, it should either ask the staff to avail itself of the best testing materials or it should call in an expert to administer a testing program and report his findings. But such professional decisions must not be made without the participation and advice of the rabbi, the educational director and the faculty.

7 A Creed for the School Board Member

The following creed for the School Board member was published by the American Association of School Administrators in their Seventeenth Yearbook, *Schools in Small Communities,* 1939. It applies equally to the member of the congregational School Board. It is reprinted with minor adaptations by permission of the publisher.

a *As a Member of the School Board—*

I will listen.

I will recognize the integrity of my predecessors and associates and the merit of their work.

I will be motivated only by a desire to serve the children of the school.

I will recognize that it is my responsibility, together with that of my fellow Board members, to see that the school is properly run—not to run it myself.

I will work through the administrative employees of the Board—not over and around them.

I will recognize that school business may be legally transacted only in open meeting legally called.

I will not "play politics"!

I will attempt to inform myself on the proper duties and functions of a School Board member.

b *In Performing the Proper Functions of a School Board Member—*

I will deal in terms of general educational policies.

I will function, in meeting the responsibility that is mine, as a part of a legislative, policy-forming body —not as an administrative officer.

I will consider myself a trustee of Jewish education and will attempt to protect and conserve it.

c *In Maintaining Desirable Relations with Other Members of the Board—*

I will respect the opinions of others.

I will recognize that authority rests with the Board in legal session—not in individual members of the Board.

I will make no disparaging remarks in or out of meeting about other members of the Board or their opinions.

I will recognize that to promise in advance of a meeting how I will vote on any proposition which is to be considered is to close my mind and agree not to think through other facts and points of view which may be presented in the meeting.

I will make decisions in Board meeting only after all sides of the question have been presented.

I will consider unethical and will thus avoid "star chamber" or "secret" sessions of Board members held without presence of the school administration.

d *In Meeting My Responsibility to My Congregation—*

I will attempt to appraise fairly both the present and the future educational needs of the congregation and the Jewish community.

I will attempt to procure adequate financial support for the school.

I will interpret to the school as best I can the needs and attitudes of the congregation, the parents, and the Jewish community.

I will consider it an important responsibility of the Board to interpret the aims and methods of the school and the materials used in it to the congregation, the parents and the Jewish community.

I will insist that business transactions of the School Board be on an ethical, open, and aboveboard basis.

e *In Working with the Educational Director and His Staff—*

I will hold the educational director responsible for the administration of the school.

I will give the educational director authority commensurate with his responsibility.

I will expect the school to be administered by the best trained technical and professional people it is possible to procure.

I will elect employees only on recommendation of the educational director, the rabbi and the consultant of the Bureau of Jewish Education.

I will participate in Board legislation only after considering the recommendation of the educational director and only after he has furnished complete information supporting his recommendation.

I will expect the educational director to keep the School Board adequately informed at all times through both oral and written reports.

I will expect to spend more time in Board meetings on educational programs and procedures than on business detail.

I will give the educational director friendly counsel and advice.

I will refer all complaints to the educational director or insist that they be presented in writing to the School Board as a whole.

I will present my personal criticisms of employees to the educational director.

I will provide adequate safeguards around the educational director and other personnel so they may perform the proper functions of education on a professional basis.

CHAPTER 5

Organizational Pattern of the Congregational School Board

Principles are mere abstractions unless there is an organization with a *modus operandi* through which these principles can be channeled. It is therefore important for the School Board not only to know its functions and the principles governing its relationships, but to know how to organize itself and how to arrange its affairs so that its business may be transacted efficiently.

1 Qualifications for School Board Membership

Many School Boards have established membership qualifications which are not directly related to the functions of the Board. For example, some School Boards recruit their members exclusively from the congregational Board of Directors. Others boast that their membership consists exclusively of parents. Still others are proud of the fact that their members are all college graduates. None of these criteria is valid. Membership on the Synagogue Board, being a parent, or possessing a Ph.D. does not necessarily qualify a person for membership on the School Board. Experience indicates that sometimes a person who is neither blessed with children nor with a formal education may prove to be quite an asset. The most important qualifications for School Board membership are the following:

a A love and understanding of children and of their needs as Jewish children.

b A devotion to Jewish education, based on a deep conviction of its importance and centrality in the synagogue program.

c A sense of values based on positive attitudes to Jewish learning and religious beliefs and practices; and a personal commitment to Jewish responsibilities in America and overseas.

d An understanding of what constitutes Jewish education and the possession of some background knowledge.

e An understanding of the functions of a School Board and one's duties as a member.

f A willingness and ability to give time and energy to the School Board's manifold activities.

g Sound judgment in evaluating many-faceted problems.

2 Size of the School Board

In the field of general education tested experience indicates that the small School Board is to be preferred for the following reasons:

a A small School Board transacts its business more expeditiously.

b A small School Board makes it possible for every member to participate in the Board's transactions, a participation which makes for ready acceptance of responsibilities. In a large School Board only a few can participate. Otherwise the meetings are prolonged and burdensome.

c A small School Board acts on all matters before it, thus giving every item of business due consideration. A large School Board has the tendency to break up into committees, with the result that the Board merely approves committee reports, often in a routine manner.

Because of these considerations, School Boards in the general field of education have become progressively smaller. According to most recent statistics most of them consist of five to nine members. Educators regard seven as the optimum number for an effective School Board.

Since the congregational School Board finds it desirable
to establish liaison with the subsidiary organizations of
the synagogue, it is necessary to enlarge the School Board.
It might be well to limit the Board to thirteen members,
consisting of seven representatives from the congregational Board of Directors, and two representatives from
each of the following organizations: the Sisterhood, the
Men's Club, and the Parent-Teacher Association.

3 Selection of School Board Members

Usually the president of the congregation and the pres-
idents of the subsidiary organizations appoint their representatives to the School Board. However, some people
feel that the members of the School Board should be
elected by their respective organizations. Those who prefer this procedure claim that elected members show a
greater sense of responsibility and develop a deeper interest in the school program. Actually it matters little
whether the School Board is appointed or elected. What
does matter is that the right people be chosen, and that
the congregation be made aware of their noteworthy contribution to the synagogue.

4 Tenure of Office

It is important that the School Board should have stability and continuity. Stability can be achieved through

long terms of office, and continuity can be achieved through a revolving membership. It is also essential for a School Board to renew its youthful vigor by replacing inactive with active members. It has therefore been found wise that:

a The tenure of each member should be at least four years.

b Only one-fourth of the membership should stand for election annually.

c A School Board member be permitted to succeed himself only once or twice.

Since some members remain useful at the expiration of their maximum term, it is wise to retain such people as honorary members with full voting rights.

No School Board can function effectively unless its members regularly participate in its transactions. Hence it is imperative that there be an on-going sifting process so as to eliminate chronic absentees. Some School Boards have found it practical to include in their bylaws a stipulation that anyone absent one-third of the year's meetings loses his membership. If this law is enforced the School Board will in time consist of people who take their duties seriously.

5 *The Officers and Committees of the School Board*

The officers of a School Board usually consist of a chairman, a vice-chairman, a secretary, and a treasurer. These officers are elected by the School Board annually, preferably during the last Board meeting of the school year, before the onset of the summer vacation.

It is advisable to have rotation in office. No one should be permitted to hold office for more than three or four consecutive years. Without such a provision in the bylaws some offices will inevitably become life jobs, with resulting stagnation.

a *Qualifications and Functions of the Chairman.* The efficiency of a School Board depends, in large measure, on its chairman. It is therefore important that the chairman, in addition to the regular qualifications for School Board membership, be able to preside over a deliberative body and know how to apply the rules of parliamentary procedure. He should be able to apply these rules tactfully but firmly. He should not rush the meeting; he should give each member an opportunity to express himself freely. But he should not permit members to speak without being recognized, nor should he permit members to speak on irrelevant subjects. The chairman should be a person who knows his functions and does not exceed his powers. His functions are primarily to preside at School Board meetings, appoint temporary and standing committees, and carry out decisions of the Board. His functions do not include the making of decisions nor the setting of policy. These belong to the Board exclusively.

Since it is important to have a strong liaison between the School Board and the Congregational Board, the bylaws should provide that the chairman of the School Board always be a member of the Congregational Board.

It is also important that the chairman be readily accessible to the rabbi and the educational director, since he must often be consulted on matters of policy between School Board meetings.

b *Functions of the Other Officers. The vice-chairman* must be ready to assume the chairman's functions whenever the latter is absent. He must therefore possess the same qualifications as the chairman. Many School Boards have made it mandatory for the vice-chairman to succeed the chairman upon the expiration of the latter's term of office. Such a provision necessitates great care in the choice of vice-chairman and precludes this office becoming merely honorary in nature.

The secretary should be provided with adequate clerical assistance. Some School Boards arrange for a stenographer to attend meetings and take minutes. This assures that the exact wording of motions will be recorded. The minutes of the meeting should be mimeographed and mailed to the School Board members several days in advance of the succeeding meeting. Such a procedure facilitates the transaction of unfinished business, since members will have refreshed their memories and given some thought to the items before they are brought up for action.

The treasurer should be elected from among the members of the School Board. Although his duties usually do not involve the collection and disbursement of school funds—these functions are generally administered by the congregational office—he is nonetheless charged with supervision of the school budget and the necessary record keeping which this function involves. Since this is a burdensome task, the treasurer should be supplied with clerical help.

All school funds should be deposited in a bank and their disbursement should always be by check. School Boards have found it wise to authorize three members as co-signers, but only two signatures should suffice for the validation of a check. The choice of co-signers should be based on convenience. However, the treasurer should always be one of them.

c *Standing Committees.* If a School Board is large its functions will necessarily be carried out through standing committees. But the disadvantage of standing committees is that they sometimes tend to usurp the powers and functions of the educational director. Also, they create duplication of effort, since the educational director makes his recommendations to the standing committees who in turn report these recommendations to the School Board. It is more practical for the educational director to make his recommendations directly to the School Board. Furthermore, as has been stated above, standing committees tend to reduce the School Board itself to the status of a rubber stamp, since the

Board tends to act upon their recommendations with little deliberation. However, if a School Board prefers to function through standing committees despite these disadvantages, the following committees have been found to be useful: (1) faculty and other personnel; (2) high school and pre-school departments; (3) library; (4) parent education and public relations; (5) scholarships and awards; (6) finances. If there is a separate school building, a committee on building and grounds is practical.

Temporary committees have often been found necessary, particularly in regard to the investigation of important matters of policy. Such special committes should make their investigations in collaboration with the educational director and report their findings to the School Board.

6 School Board Meetings

It is essential that the School Board meet regularly. A School Board that meets only when the chairman or the educational director has business to transact inevitably becomes an impotent body. Most School Boards meet once a month on a set date. Additional or special meetings should be called at the discretion of the chairman.

The meetings should begin promptly and should not be allowed to drag to late hours. A chairman who keeps the discussion to items on the agenda and does not allow digression usually succeeds in transacting the business in two hours or less. Experience indicates that the business of the meeting is transacted more expeditiously if the agenda is mailed to members in advance of the meeting.

The order of business should be as follows:

a *Preliminaries.*

Call to Order. As soon as a quorum is available and the official time of the meeting has arrived, the chairman calls the meeting to order. (The number of members constituting a quorum should be decided by the School Board and should be included in its bylaws.)

Roll Call. It is advisable to keep a careful record of attendance. This will prove helpful at the end of the year when the parent bodies can be informed of their representatives' regularity or irregularity of attendance.

b *Approval of Minutes.* If the minutes were mailed to members in advance, this item is mere routine unless there are corrections to be made.

c *Report by Rabbi, Educational Director or Principal.* This report usually determines the agenda of the meeting, since it includes not only a summary of school events but also communications, unfinished business and recommended new business. (If the Board functions through committees, their reports precede or supplant the report by the professional executive.)

d *Correspondence.*

e *Unfinished Business.*

f *New Business.*

g *Adjournment.*

The parliamentary procedures of the meetings should be simple. Complex rules are often confusing and lead to as much chaos as does the absence of all rules. It is well to remember that the goal of all School Board meetings is to arrive at a meeting of minds rather than to decide matters by majority rule. This rule is an important technique in democratic procedure. But a meeting of minds is the essence of a democratic deliberative body. If questions on parliamentary procedure arise they should be settled by referral to a standard book on parliamentary law such as *Robert's Rules of Order.*

7 Record Keeping

An efficiently organized School Board maintains accurate records of its transactions and of school developments. The most important of these records are (1) minute book, (2) code of rules and regulations, (3) periodic reports and (4) school calendar.

a *School Board Minutes.* The minutes of each meeting should be carefully recorded and kept in a loose leaf book, in a place accessible to Board members. Minutes should be complete and accurate, since they are the official record of the Board's activities. It has been found practical to leave a wide margin on the left side of the sheet. In this margin titles of resolutions are noted. Some people prefer to place these titles at the head of each resolution as paragraph headings. By keeping the minutes in this form, it is always possible to locate a resolution by merely glancing down these marginal or paragraph headlines. Appendix D is a sample of School Board minutes taken from the minute book of a well functioning congregational school.

b *Code of Rules and Regulations.* Since a School Board concerns itself with setting school policies, it is advisable that these policies be recorded not only in the minutes but separately as well. The compilation of these policy records is usually known as the Code of Rules and Regulations. It is a handy guide to the authoritative rulings and guiding principles by which the school is governed. The Code is a kind of constitution governing matters of dispute that are brought to the attention of the educational director or the School Board. This Code should be kept up to date, should be on hand at every meeting, and should always be accessible to Board members for reference.

c *School Reports.* A well informed School Board is usually a well functioning Board. A member who knows what is going on in the school and is aware of the problems confronting the educational director is usually an interested member, ready to contribute his thinking and his efforts. Hence it is important for the educational director to supply the School Board with periodic reports. These may be monthly attendance reports, periodic financial reports, annual reports on the whole educational program, etc. Such reports should be carefully filed for future reference.

d *School Calendar.* A well functioning school publishes its calendar for the school year long before the opening of school. This calendar lists the dates of registration, school opening and closing, school holidays, special school events, public school vacations, etc. Appendix E is a reprint of the School Calendar for 1951–2, drawn up by one of our better schools. Every member of the Board should be provided with the school calendar.

The organizational pattern of the congregational school as outlined in this chapter is necessarily sketchy. Much is left to the good common sense of the School Board which usually consists of men and women with organizational experience. Sketchy as this pattern is, however, it can prove of great value if its suggestions, based on wide experience both in the general and the Jewish educational fields, are taken seriously and followed consistently. Needless to say, the suggestions should be adapted to the local situation. Such adaptation will definitely add to the usefulness of the organizational pattern.

CONCLUSION

תֶּחֱזַקְנָה יְדֵיכֶם

"Let Your Hands Be Strong"

It has been said that "some Jews wear their Judaism as a badge, while to others it is a stamp, stamped on their very souls." The former spend their lives talking about anti-Semitism and fighting real or imaginary anti-Semites; the latter live their Judaism and, because their lives reflect the beauty and holiness of their heritage, they fulfill the prophetic destiny of the Jew to be "God's witnesses" and "a blessing." It is from the ranks of such Jews that members of congregational School Boards are usually recruited.

Jews whose Judaism is "stamped on their very souls" are deeply concerned with all phases of Jewish life. Their concern is motivated by a bright vision of the American

Jewish community, a vision which they sense but cannot articulate. It was the late Professor Israel Friedlander, of blessed memory, who succinctly articulated this vision in the following memorable words:

> We perceive a community great in numbers, mighty in power, enjoying life, liberty and the pursuit of happiness: true life, not mere breathing space; full liberty, not mere elbow room; real happiness, not that of pasture beasts; actively participating in the civic, social and economic progress of the country, . . . yet deeply rooted in the soil of Judaism, clinging to its past, working for its future, true to its traditions, faithful to its aspirations, one in sentiment with their brethren wherever they are, attached to the land of their fathers as the cradle and resting place of the Jewish spirit; men with straight backs and raised heads, with big hearts and strong minds, with no conviction crippled, with no emotion stifled, . . . not a formless crowd of taxpayers and voters, but a sharply marked community, distinct and distinguished, trusted for its loyalty, respected for its dignity, esteemed for its traditions, valued for its aspirations, a community such as the Prophet of the Exile saw it in his vision: "And marked will be their seed among the nations, and their offspring among the peoples. Everyone that will see them will point to them as a community blessed by the Lord." (Quoted in *Modern Jewish Life in Literature* by Azriel Eisenberg, United Synagogue Commission on Jewish Education, New York, 1948, pp. 216-17.)

Such a vision brightens the eyes of the loyal and devoted Jew. The American Jewish community, with its many ideological shadings, thus appears beautiful and promising.

But there are occasions when he sees the American Jewish community as an autumn tree, beautiful in its russet foliage but with many of its leaves carried off by the wind. The tree is still majestic, but the sight is not reassuring. There is the ever present knowledge that the next blast will leave the tree totally bare. The sensitive Jew is aware that the first cold winds have already passed over American Jewry. Is it not a fact that the last generation is generally regarded as "a lost generation"? And he is deeply worried lest his radiant vision fade with the loss of another generation.

It is because of his shining dreams for the future and the troubling fears of the present that this type of Jew logically places the highest priority on the Jewish education of his child. He fully appreciates the wisdom of Moses who chose to teach the Torah before building the Tabernacle. As a member of the synagogue he, too, resolves that of all the congregational activities the school should have first priority. His motto becomes the rabbinic teaching that "the beneficent effects of a number of pious acts are eternal but תַּלְמוּד תּוֹרָה כְּנֶגֶד כֻּלָּם—the teaching of the Torah exceeds them all."

What kind of Jewish education does this type of Jew want for the Jewish child? It is an education not measured in dollars but in terms of the lofty vision that inspires and directs his own daily strivings. He wants Jewish education to be like "the tree of the field." Its roots are to be deep, i.e., an education that is intensive and maximal; its stem is to be tall, i.e., an education extending from early childhood through the entire life span; its trunk is to be sturdy, i.e., an education that is strengthened by a trained and devoted faculty; and its crown is to be broad, i.e., an education reaching out to more and more of our children.

It is out of the ranks of such Jews that the School Board enrolls its members, and it is into the hands of these men that the Jewish education of our children is entrusted. It is to them that we address the prophetic words:

> *"Thus saith the Lord of Hosts:*
>
> תֶּחֱזַקְנָה יְדֵיכֶם
>
> *Let your hands be strong,*
>
> *Ye that hear in these days these words"* (ZECH. 8.9).

Appendices

APPENDIX A *Sample Congregational School Budget*

Proposed Budget for Beth El Hebrew School
FISCAL YEAR—SEPT. 1, 1951—AUG. 31, 1952

	Income Sept. 1, 1950 to Apr. 30, 1951	Anticipated Income May 1, 1951 to Aug. 31, 1951	Total Income Sept. 1, 1950 to Aug. 31, 1951	Anticipated Income Sept. 1, 1951 to Aug. 31, 1952
Tuition (Hebrew School)	6,975.	1,200.	8,175.	8,500.
Tuition (Nursery School)	5,400.	—	5,400.	5,550.
Congregation Allocation	9,000.	—	9,000.	10,000.
Books	1,075.	75.	1,150.	1,300.
Transportation	640.	90.	730.	750.
Sisterhood Scholarships	1,000.	—	1,000.	1,000.
Men's Club	325.	—	325.	400.
Parent-Teacher Association	725.	—	725.	1,000.
Total	25,140.	1,365.	26,505.	28,500.

	Expenditures Sept. 1, 1950 to Apr. 30, 1951	Anticipated Expenditures May 1, 1951 to Aug. 31, 1951	Total Expenditures Sept. 1, 1950 to Aug. 31, 1951	Anticipated Expenditures Sept. 1, 1951 to Aug. 31, 1952
Salaries:				
Principal	4,333.34	2,166.66	6,500.	7,000.
Teacher A	2,400.00	1,200.00	3,600.	3,800.
Teacher B	2,200.00	1,100.00	3,300.	3,500.
Teacher C	2,066.66	1,033.34	3,100.	3,300.
Nursery Teacher	2,200.00	1,100.00	3,300.	3,500.
Asst. Nurs. Teacher	800.00	400.00	1,200.	1,400.
4 Sunday Sch. Teachers	666.66	333.34	1,000.	1,000.
Pensions and Insurance	980.00	490.00	1,470.	1,575.
Books and Materials	1,740.00	—	1,740.	2,000.
Holiday Observances	255.00	45.00	300.	350.
Jr. Congr. and Other Extra-Curr. Activities	625.00	150.00	775.	800.
Transportation	875.00	225.00	1,100.	1,200.
Office and Misc. Exp.	215.00	35.00	250.	300.
Accident Insurance	125.00	—	125.	125.
Reserves	—	115.00	115.	125.
Total	19,481.66	8,393.34	27,875.	29,975.

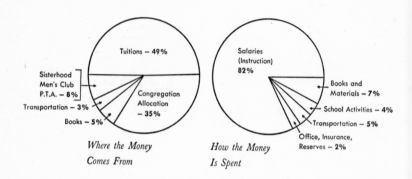

Where the Money
Comes From

How the Money
Is Spent

Codes of Practice

1 *Code of Practice for Jewish Schools* [For the guidance of Hebrew Schools in New York City in regulating the relations between teachers and schools]. Adopted by the Board of Review, May 1944 and revised March 1947. Published by the Jewish Education Committee of New York (1776 Broadway, New York 19, N. Y.).

2 *Code of Practice for Jewish Schools* [Governing employment and services of principals, and regulating the relations between principals and Hebrew schools]. Adopted by the Board of Review, February 1952. Published by the Jewish Education Committee of New York (1776 Broadway, New York 19, N. Y.).

3 *Code of Practice for Principals and Teachers in Bureau-Affiliated Schools,* Revised edition, November 1948. Published by the Bureau of Jewish Education of the Los Angeles Jewish Community Council (560 North Vermont Ave., Los Angeles 4, Calif.).

4 *Code of Administrative and Personnel Practices*—Adopted by the Allied Jewish School Board, June 1948 and amended in March 1951. Published by the Chicago Board of Jewish Education (72 East 11th Street, Chicago 5, Ill.).

5 *Code of Personnel Practices for Sunday School Teachers*—Adopted by the Allied Jewish School Board, January 1952. Published by the Chicago Board of Jewish Education (72 East 11th St., Chicago 5, Ill.).

6 *New Haven Hebrew Teachers Code of Practice*—Approved May 1950. Published by the New Haven Bureau of Jewish Education (152 Temple St., New Haven, Conn.).

7 *Code of Practice for the Hebrew Schools of Greater Boston* [Covering qualifications of teachers, employment services, security of teachers, and controversies, conciliation, arbitration and appeal]. Adopted in 1947–48. Published by the Boston Bureau of Education (72 Franklin Street, Boston 10, Mass.).

8 *Code of Practice for Jewish Schools* [A Code of Practice to guide the schools affiliated with the Philadelphia Council on Jewish Education in their relations with their teachers and in the settlement of controversies within schools]. Adopted March, 1948. Also *Frame of Reference* [Rules and regulations, classification of teachers, and salary schedules pertaining to teachers in elementary week-day schools]. Adopted by the Community Board of License, September, 1948. Published by the Philadelphia Council on Jewish Education (1011 Chestnut St., Philadelphia, Pa.).

Bureau and Congregational
School Relationships

*A Statement of Principles Adopted by the United Syna-
gogue Commission on Jewish Education and the American Association for Jewish Education (1950–5710).*

1 We recognize that the perpetuation and enrichment of Jewish
life in America will in large measure be decided by the char-
acter of Jewish education that we provide for our children.
We further realize that in order to achieve an adequate system of Jewish education it is imperative that all forces dedi-
cated to the achievement of this goal cooperate fully and
wholeheartedly. We, the United Synagogue Commission on
Jewish Education and the American Association for Jewish
Education, therefore join in issuing this statement on the cooperation of congregational schools and Bureaus of Jewish
Education. We also resolve to study the respective areas of our
work with the view to define areas of cooperation and to plan
the implementation of such cooperative efforts on a nation-
wide scale. Since not all areas in Jewish education have been
covered by this statement, it is desirable that additional discussions take place between the United Synagogue Commission and the American Association to supplement this statement and to discover additional areas of cooperative effort.

2 The past quarter of a century has witnessed an increase in the
number of central educational agencies commonly known as

Bureaus of Jewish Education. Similarly, there has been a rise in the number of congregational schools. Both increases were brought on by special needs of the American Jewish community. Both the Bureaus and the congregational schools can contribute greatly to the well-being of American Jewry.

3 Bureaus should recognize and accept the existence of congregational schools and of organized groups of congregational schools as a logical concomitant of American Jewish life. In consonance with their philosophy of encouraging, promoting and extending the program of all educational agencies and segments in the community, the Bureaus should cooperate with the congregational schools or their groupings in carrying out their programs as effectively as possible.

The congregational schools should accept the Bureaus as the central community instruments for educational coordination and consultation in terms of improving standards of achievement and progress.

4 For the purpose of effective cooperation between the congregational schools and the Bureaus, it is imperative that the following principles which have proved effective in many communities be regarded as basic:

a The Bureaus, as central community agencies, shall at all times recognize the autonomy and the ideological integrity of the congregational schools.

b Whatever services a Bureau renders to any one ideological group it must be prepared to grant to all ideological groups.

c Whenever congregational school units are too small to be effective, the Bureau may take the initiative to encourage congregational and other schools of similar types to pool their efforts with the end in view of operating a common school. It is understood that the rabbi will cooperate with the program and the effective operation of the consolidated school. However, he should be given the opportunity to guide the religious growth and experience of the children of the congregation of which he is the spiritual leader.

5 Congregational schools should be encouraged to provide educational facilities for their children from the pre-school through the high school level. In the event that a congregational school is not equipped or is too small to be effective, or is otherwise unable to undertake this responsibility, either in the pre-school or the high school area, and if there does not exist a local congregational school system prepared to assume this responsibility, the Bureau should undertake to carry on such an activity with the full cooperation of the school involved. The Bureau, however, should help the congregational school mature to its responsibility for the conduct of its own pre-school and high school program. However, if a community high school now exists, the congregational school should make every effort to cooperate with that community high school before it decides to establish a high school of its own.

6 It is hoped that this statement, which was drafted by the American Association for Jewish Education and the United Synagogue Commission on Jewish Education, will be implemented in a spirit of mutual faith and wholehearted cooperation so that the sacred duty of teaching the Torah to our children may be effectively fulfilled.

For The United Synagogue
Commission on Jewish Education
  Elias Charry
  Moshe Davis
  Leo L. Honor
  Abraham E. Millgram

For the American Association
for Jewish Education
  Azriel Eisenberg
  A. P. Gannes
  Judah Pilch
  David Rudavsky

APPENDIX D

Sample Minutes of a Congregational School Board Meeting

Minutes of the Beth El School Board Meeting

City of ....

Tuesday evening, Jan. 16, 1951

The Beth El School Board met in regular session in the Social Room of the school building on Jan. 16, 1951. The meeting was called to order at 8 P.M. by the chairman, Mr. Herman Frank. In the absence of the secretary, Mrs. H. Berman, the chairman appointed Mr. L. Friedman to read the minutes of the previous meeting and to serve as acting secretary.

Roll Call

Present

Rabbi Goldman; Messrs. Frank, Goodman, Friedman, Warsau, Miller, Jacobs; Mesdames Halpern, Aronson, and the Educational Director, Mr. Leonard.

Absent

Mrs. H. Berman.

Reading and Approval of Minutes

Disposition of Minutes

The minutes of the last meeting which was held on Dec. 19, 1950 were previously mailed to each member of the Board. The minutes were approved as mailed.

Educational Director's Report

Report of
Ed. Dir.

Mr. Leonard, the Educational Director, rendered his monthly report on the activities and events that took place in the school since the last School Board meeting. The following were the high lights:

Registration

1. To date there are 265 pupils enrolled in the school of whom 76 are in the primary grades, 125 in the Elementary Department, 48 in the Jr. High School Department, and 16 in the High School Department.

Jr. Cong.
and Choir

2. Members of the Junior Congregation and the choir will conduct the Late Friday Evening Service in the main synagogue on Friday, January 26, with their own rabbi, cantor and choir officiating. Members of the School Board were urged to attend these special services.

Tu Bishvat
Celebration

3. The annual Tu Bishvat celebration will take place on Monday, Jan. 22. The P.T.A. will provide the pupils with bags of fruit from Israel.

Open
School
Week

4. Open School Week will take place next week. Parents will be served tea by the P.T.A. before visiting the classes. As part of Open School Week there will be a parents meeting featuring a symposium in which two parents and two members of the School Board will discuss "How Our New Building Can Best Serve the Jewish Community."

Requirements
for
Confirmation

5. The Educational Director suggested that the School Board consider a change in the requirements for Confirmation. He recommended that Confirmation be limited to graduates of the High School Department. The matter is to be taken up at a future meeting of the Board.

Unfinished Business

Nursery
School

Mrs. Aronson announced that the opening of the Nursery School was approved by the Congregational Board of Trustees, and that the rabbi had announced the project from the pulpit. Twenty-two inquiries have already been received. Mr. Leonard submitted in writing facts and figures on six nursery schools as guides in the administration and financing of the nursery school. The report is herewith attached. Mrs. Halpern suggested that immediate action be taken so as to enable the School Board to publicize this project and engage teachers. A subcommittee consisting of Messrs. Warsau, Miller and Mrs. Aronson, was appointed to review the plan and to bring in recommendations at the next meeting of the Board.

New Business

Bar Mitzvah
Preparation

The matter of Bar Mitzvah preparation in relation to the curriculum was brought up for discussion by the Educational Director. This matter will also be discussed at the next School Board meeting which is to be held on Tuesday, February 20, in the Social Room of the School Building.

Communications

P.T.A.

Serving Refreshments to
Pupils Before
Class

Mr. Leonard presented a communication from Mrs. H. Siegel, President of the P.T.A., suggesting that the school serve milk and cookies to the children before class. The P.T.A. is willing to furnish the milk and cookies as well as a committee of volunteers to supervise the serving. It was decided to accept the suggestion with thanks. The Educational Director was authorized to communicate with Mrs. Siegel and to implement this project.

Regional
Educational
Conference

Mr. Leonard read a communication from the United Synagogue Commission on Jewish Education announcing that a Regional Educational Conference will be held on Sunday, March 18, 1951, at Temple Beth Abraham, ... City. Mr. Leonard explained the organization and the program of the Conference and asked every member of the School Board to attend. He also suggested that the school defray the expenses of the faculty so as to encourage them to attend. Every member of the Board pledged attendance. The School Board also authorized the payment of all expenses for members of the faculty attending the Conference. The Educational Director was asked to invite the Board of Trustees and the Boards of all affiliated organizations to attend this Conference.

Adjournment

The meeting was adjourned at 10:30 P.M.

Respectfully submitted,

....

L. Friedman
Acting Secretary

Sample School Calendar

School Calender 1951–52 (5712)

Monday	Elul 2	September 3	Labor Day
Tuesday-Sunday	Elul 3-8	September 4-9	School Registration
Wednesday-Thursday	Elul 4-5	September 5-6	Teachers Seminars
Monday	Elul 9	September 10	School Opens
Saturday	Elul 14	September 15	First Junior Congregation Service
Sunday	Elul 15	September 16	First Session of Kindergarten Class
Sunday	Elul 22	September 23	Late Registration Closes
Wednesday	Elul 25	September 26	School Board Meeting
Sunday	Elul 29	September 30	Erev Rosh Hashanah Regular Sessions
Monday-Tuesday	Tishri 1-2	October 1-2	Rosh Hashanah
Tuesday	Tishri 9	October 9	Erev Yom Kippur No Sessions
Wednesday	Tishri 10	October 10	Yom Kippur
Sunday	Tishri 14	October 14	Erev Sukkot Regular Sessions
Monday-Tuesday	Tishri 15-16	October 15-16	Sukkot

Wednesday- Thursday	Tishri 17-18	October 17-18	School Parties in Sukkah
Sunday	Tishri 21	October 21	Erev Sukkot Regular Sessions
Monday	Tishri 22	October 22	Shemini Atzeret
Tuesday	Tishri 23	October 23	Simhat Torah Consecration Service
Wednesday	Tishri 24	October 24	First Junior Choir Session
Monday- Tuesday	Tishri 29-30	October 29-30	Junior Congregation Elections
Friday	Heshvan 3	November 2	Balfour Day
Tuesday	Heshvan 7	November 6	Election Day Morning Sessions
Sunday	Heshvan 19	November 18	Fall Inter-School Assembly
Thursday	Heshvan 23	November 22	Thanksgiving Day No Sessions
Wednesday	Heshvan 29	November 28	School Board Meeting
Wednesday- Thursday	Heshvan 29-30	November 28-29	Report Card Distri- bution
Sunday	Kislev 3	December 2	Fall Inter-School Panel Discussion
Sunday	Kislev 24	December 23	First Hanukah Candle Annual Hanukah Celebration
Monday- Monday	Kislev 25- Tevet 2	December 24-31	Hanukah
Wednesday- Thursday	Kislev 27-28	December 26-27	Class Hanukah Parties
Sunday- Tuesday	Tevet 1-3	December 30- January 1	Hanukah Vacation
Monday- Friday	Tevet 23-27	January 21-25	Midyear Inter-School Examinations for First Year Class

Wednesday	Tevet 25	January 23	School Board Meeting
Monday	Shevat 15	February 11	Tu Bishvat Regular Sessions
Tuesday	Shevat 16	February 12	Lincoln's Birthday Morning Sessions
Sunday	Adar 12	March 9	Purim Celebration
Monday	Adar 13	March 10	Erev Purim Megillah Service for Children
Tuesday	Adar 14	March 11	Purim No Sessions
Wednesday	Adar 29	March 26	School Board Meeting
Sunday	Nisan 4	March 30	Spring Inter-School Panel Discussion
Wednesday- Thursday	Nisan 7-8	April 2-3	Report Card Distri- bution
Sunday	Nisan 11	April 6	School Model Seder
Wednesday	Nisan 14	April 9	Erev Pesaḥ No Sessions
Thursday- Thursday	Nisan 15-22	April 10-17	Pesaḥ No Sessions
Friday- Friday	Nisan 16-23	April 11-18	Public School Spring Vacation
Wednesday	Iyar 5	April 30	Israel Independence Day
Tuesday	Iyar 18	May 13	Lag Ba-Omer Regular Sessions
Sunday	Iyar 23	May 18	Lag Ba-Omer Outing
Wednesday	Sivan 4	May 28	School Board Meeting
Thursday	Sivan 5	May 29	Erev Shavuot No Sessions
Friday	Sivan 6	May 30	1st day Shavuot Confirmation Service
Saturday	Sivan 7	May 31	2nd day Shavuot

Sunday	Sivan 8	June 1	Arts Festival
Thursday	Sivan 19	June 12	Final Examinations Begin
Wednesday	Sivan 25	June 18	Inter-School Reception to Graduates
Thursday	Sivan 26	June 19	School Closes Closing Assembly

BIBLIOGRAPHY

Carpenter, W. W., Capps, A. G., and Townsend, L. G., *Suggestions for Procedure for Missouri Boards of Education,* University of Missouri, Columbia, Mo., 1948.

"Choosing the Superintendent of Schools," American Association of School Administrators, 1949.

Deffenbough, W. S., "Practices and Concepts Relating to City Boards of Education" in *Biennial Survey of Education in the United States,* Vol. I, Chapter VII, Federal Security Agency, United States Office of Education, Washington, 1941.

Engelman, Uriah Z. and Horowitz, Morris C., *Tuition Fees in Weekday Afternoon Schools,* American Association for Jewish Education, New York, 1952.

Gibbs, Andrew H., "Criteria for Selecting School Board Members" in *Education for Victory,* 3:3-4, 20, April 20, 1945.

"Lay Leadership" in *Schools in Small Communities,* Seventeenth Yearbook of the American Assn. of School Administrators (a department of the N.E.A.), Washington, D. C., 1939, pp. 309-333.

Millgram, Abraham E., "Can the American City and County School Boards Provide a Pattern for the Congregational School Board?" in *The Synagogue School,* Vol. XI, No. 2 (November 1952), pp. 2-7.

Mort, Paul R., *Principles of School Administration,* McGraw-Hill Book Company, New York, 1946, Chapters XVIII and XIX, pp. 280-324.

The Objectives and Standards for the Congregational School, United Synagogue Commission on Jewish Education, New York, 1948.

Ruffman, Louis L. and Goldberg, Henry R., "The Job of the Principal" in *The Pedagogic Reporter,* Vol. IV, No. 2 (November 1952), American Association for Jewish Education, N. Y.

School Boards in Action, Twenty-fourth Yearbook of the American Assn. of School Administrators (a department of the N.E.A.), Washington, D. C., 1946.

The School Board Member, Research Division, N.E.A., Res. B. 11:1-41, Washington, D. C., 1933.

Sorenson, Ray, *The Art of Board Membership,* Association Press, New York, 1950.

Status and Practices of Boards of Education, Research Division, N.E.A., Res. B. 24:47-83, Washington, D. C., 1936.

United Synagogue Commission on Jewish Education

Elias Charry,
CHAIRMAN
Josiah Derby,
VICE-CHAIRMAN
Louis L. Ruffman,
SECRETARY
Hyman Chanover

George Ende
Azriel Eisenberg
Sylvia C. Ettenberg
Henry R. Goldberg
A. Hillel Henkin
Leo L. Honor
Ario S. Hyams
Harold Kastle

Alter F. Landesman
Harry O. H. Levine
Stanley Rabinowitz
Zevi Scharfstein
Simon Shoop
Abraham Simon
Samuel Sussman

Judah Goldin, *Dean, Teachers Institute, Jewish Theological Seminary*
Simon Greenberg, *Executive Director, United Synagogue of America*
Wolfe Kelman, *Executive Secretary, Rabbinical Assembly of America*
Abraham E. Millgram, *Educational Director, United Synagogue of America*

Committee on Textbook Publications

Henry R. Goldberg,
CHAIRMAN
Barnet Cohen
Josiah Derby

Morris S. Goodblatt
Solomon Grayzel
Leon Lang
Harry O. H. Levine

Isidore S. Meyer
Abraham E. Millgram
Louis Newman

107